Cells, Tiss Organs & Systems

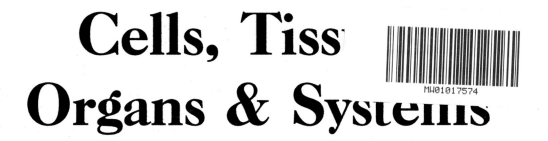

MW01017574

Grades 7-8

Written by Sandra Appleby
Illustrated by Ric Ward

ISBN 978-1-55035-652-6
Copyright 1999
Revised January 2007
All Rights Reserved * Printed in Canada

Published in the United States by:
On The Mark Press
3909 Witmer Road PMB 175
Niagara Falls, New York
14305
www.onthemarkpress.com

Published in Canada by:
S&S Learning Materials
15 Dairy Avenue
Napanee, Ontario
K7R 1M4
www.sslearning.com

© On The Mark Press • S&S Learning Materials

OTM-2107 • SSB1-107 Cells, Tissues, Organs & Systems

At  Glance

Learning Expectations	Lessons 1 to 5	Lessons 6 to 11	Lessons 12 to 16	Lessons 17 to 22
Understanding Concepts				
• Identify unicellular (e.g., bacteria) and multicellular (e.g., humans) organisms	•			
• Compare the basic needs of unicellular organisms to those of humans	•			
• Identify the parts of a cell (e.g., organelles such as nucleus, mitochondria)	•		•	
• Identify the structural differences between plant and animal cells	•			
• Describe the organization of cells into tissues, organs and systems		•		
• Demonstrate an understanding of how selectively permeable membranes function in a cell		•		
• Describe the structures and functions of specialized cells and tissues in plants (e.g., leaves, roots)		•		
• Describe how a plant's roots, stem and leaves allow movement of food, water and gases		•		
• Compare the structural adaptations of different plants and describe how these adaptations are suited for the plant's environment	•	•		
• Describe the movement of gases and water in and out of cells during diffusion and osmosis			•	
Inquiry , Design & Communication Skills				
• Use a microscope to observe and draw cells			•	
• Design and conduct and experiment to test a hypothesis on the effect of salt on plant growth			•	
• Identify the requirements to conduct a fair test			•	
• Compile qualitative and quantitative data gathered through experimentation using diagrams and charts		•	•	•
• Communicate procedures and results of investigations using oral presentations, written descriptions, charts, drawings and models	•	•	•	•
• Create a 3-dimentional model of a unicellular organism	•		•	
• Use appropriate science and technology vocabulary to communicate ideas, procedures and results	•	•	•	•
Relating Science & Technology to the World Outside the School				
• Describe ways in which the various systems in the human body are interdependent				•
• Compare the respiratory systems of plants and animals				•
• Investigate variables that affect blood pressure				•
• Investigate the differing levels of vitamin C in a variety of frozen and fresh fruit juices				•

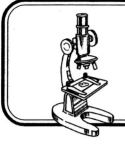

CELLS, TISSUES, ORGANS & SYSTEMS

Table of Contents

CELLS, TISSUES, ORGANS & SYSTEMS

Teacher Assessment Rubric

Student's Name: _____

Criteria	Level 1	Level 2	Level 3	Level 4	Level
Understanding Concepts					
• Demonstrated understanding of basic concepts	Limited	Some	General	Thorough	
• Characteristics of demonstrated misconceptions	Significant misconceptions	Minor misconceptions	No significant misconceptions	No misconceptions	
• Characteristics of explanations that were given	Show limited understanding of concepts	Only partial explanations given	Usually complete or almost complete	Always complete and accurate	
Inquiry & Research Skills					
• Number of required skills that were successfully applied	Few	Some	Most	All/almost all	
• Demonstrated awareness of safety procedures	Limited	Some	Good	Consistent	
• Ability to use tools and equipment correctly and independently	Needs assistance	Needs some assistance	Needs only occasional assistance	Needs little or no assistance	
Relating Science to the World Outside the School					
• Demonstrated understanding of the connections between biology and the world outside school	Limited	Some	Demonstrates understanding	Understands connections and their implications	
Communication Skills					
• Use of the correct vocabulary, and clarity and precision of communication	Limited	Some	Good	Consistent	

Comments: _____

_____

_____

_____

_____

CELLS, TISSUES, ORGANS & SYSTEMS
Student Self-Assessment Rubric

Name: _____   Date: _____

Put a check mark in each box that most accurately describes your performance, then add your points to determine your total score.

Expectations	My Performance				
	Always/almost always (4 Points)	Frequently (3 Points)	Sometimes (2 Points)	Needs Improvement (1 Point)	Points
✓ I was focused and stayed on task.					
✓ I reread portions of the material in order to understand the concepts being described.					
✓ I used all the resources available to answer questions.					
✓ My answers are thoughtful and show consistent effort.					
✓ I recorded my observations accurately and in detail.					
✓ I proofread my work for spelling, grammar, and overall clarity.					
✓ I can talk about what I learned about cells, tissues, organs and systems.					
✓ I know what I am good at.					
✓ I know what I need to work on.					

Total Points: _____

Questions for personal reflection:

1. What did you find most interesting and enjoy learning about the most?

2. What questions do you have now, and what would you like to learn more about?

3. What can you improve upon and how can you make this improvement?

CELLS, TISSUES, ORGANS & SYSTEMS

Overall Expectations

- Students will become familiar with the differences between unicellular and multicellular plant and animal cells.

- Students will have the opportunity to experience experimental design, procedure and analysis.

- Students will have the opportunity to explore the various structures involved in cellular life and the effects of outside influences upon these structures.

- Students will have the opportunity to reflect upon the importance of scientific inquiry to human health.

Introducing the Unit to Students

- On a large piece of chart paper cut out the shape of a cell, and record the students' brainstormed ideas on what a cell is made of and what a cell makes up.

- Have students work in pairs, choose a physical activity, (e.g., walking, running, reading, eating, etc.) and brainstorm all of the various systems and organs that are used during that activity.

- To demonstrate the concept of a cell, cut an orange into its sections. Compare each section with its membrane to a cell.

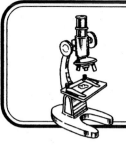

Cells, Tissues, Organs & Systems

Vocabulary

Amoeba – a unicellular organism of the protozoa variety that moves by pseudopodia

Anther – found at the end of the stamen, this organ contains pollen

Bacteria – any of many unicellular organisms of various forms; they are often the cause of disease

Bias – the tendency of the investigator to affect the outcome of the experiment through his/her preconceived notions of what that outcome might be

Bone – hard, dense tissue that provides form and support for the body and the location of red blood cell production

Buccal – to do with the cheek; the buccal cavity is the mouth

Carpel – the female flower organ that contains the ovary

Cartilage - strong elastic fibers that give structure to the nose, the ears, the epiglottis and cushions joints

Cell Membrane – a semipermeable membrane blocking unwanted substances from the cell and containing cell matter

Connective Tissue – this tissue supports or binds organs within the body cavity

Cytoplasm – the protoplasm of a cell excluding the nucleus

Deoxyribonucleic Acid (DNA) – a double – helix structure of nucleotides that contains all of a cell's genetic information

Diastole – the measure of blood pressure as the heart relaxes to refill with blood

Diffusion – the movement of molecules or ions from areas of higher concentration to areas of lower concentration

Endocrine Gland – a group of cells or an organ that makes and secretes a substance directly into the bloodstream (e.g., hormones)

Endocytosis – intake of fluids

Endoplasmic Reticulum - site of protein production; also involved in storage and transport

Engulfing – the cell process of surrounding and incorporating food or bacteria into a vacuole

Epidermis – the protective outer layer of the skin

Epithelial Tissue (Epithelium) – this tissue covers and protects the external surfaces of the body (skin) and lines its internal cavities

Equilibrium – a state of balance

Eukaryotic Cells – complex cells with a nucleus membrane; all multicellular organism are eukaryotes

CELLS, TISSUES, ORGANS & SYSTEMS

Exocrine Gland – a group of cells or an organ that makes and secretes a substance via a duct (e.g., sweat)

Exocytosis – the expulsion of cell products or cell waste

Extrapolate – to generalize or extend your findings about a small sample to a larger sample

Fair Test – the test which has been conducted without bias, has been controlled for variables, is valid, and uses a random sampling

Flagella – a hair-like, motile projection on the extremity of a protozoan or bacterium

Golgi Apparatus - a collection of sacs that store and then release compounds made in the endoplasmic reticulum

Herbacious – green and leaf-like

Hypothesis – a testable idea

Interdependence – the situation in which two or more organisms, organs or systems are dependent on each other for optimum functioning

Lysosome – an organelle in the cytoplasm of a cell which contains powerful digestive enzymes

Macrophage – a type of cell that travels through the body ingesting any foreign particles including bacteria

Meiosis – the kind of cell division which only occurs in the formation of ova and sperm, and produces daughter cells with half the number of chromosomes of the parent cell

Metabolism – consists of the physical and chemical reactions that build and maintain life

Mitochondria – the organelle that produces energy in a cell that is necessary to carry out all cell functions

Neuron – a nerve cell

Nucleus – an organelle that contains the genetic information for the cell

Organelle – a structure in a cell which has a specific purpose

Organic Compounds – composed of carbon, hydrogen, oxygen and nitrogen, these substances exist only in living things

Osmosis – the diffusion of fluid through a semi-permeable membrane

Ovary – female reproductive organ

Phagocytosis – the engulfing of food particles by a cell

Phloem – vascular tissue in plants through which food is transported throughout the plant

Pistil – the female reproductive organ of a flower

Prokaryotic Cells – cells without a nuclear membrane; bacteria are prokaryotes

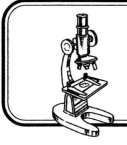 

Protozoans – a group of one-celled microorganisms

Pseudopod – the fluid, appendage-type extension of a unicellular organism

Qualitative – results based on observation that are descriptive rather than measured

Quantitative – measurable data, numbers, and statistics representing an observation

Random Sampling – a sample collected by chance

Respiration – to breathe

Ribonucleic Acid (RNA) – codes information for making proteins; this nucleic acid is found in the cell's nucleus and cytoplasm

Ribosomes – particles containing RNA responsible for making proteins; they are free floating in the cytoplasm but often are found attached to the endoplasmic reticulum

Selectively Permeable – a membrane which allows the passage of some substances but not others

Sphygmomanometer – an instrument used to measure blood pressure in millimeters of mercury

Stamen – the pollen-producing, male reproductive organ of a flower

Stigma – the top on the pistil of a flower where pollen is deposited at pollination

Stimulus – a change in the environment of an organism which elicits a response in the organism

Systole – the contraction of the heart as it empties its blood into the circulation system

Tropism – the growth response a plant has to an external stimulus

Validity – the concept that the experiment is reliable, and consistent

Variables – those characteristics about the situation which may affect the outcome of the experiment

Vesicles – small sacks found in the cytoplasm of cells; may contain various substances

Xylem – woody tissue of vascular plants that transports water and nutrients, and supports the stem

Zygote – a fertilized ovum (egg) prior to cell division

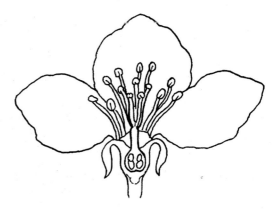

CELLS, TISSUES, ORGANS & SYSTEMS

Planning Ahead

There are several suggestions for labs and activities throughout this resource which require equipment and/or materials. Listed here is the equipment needed, organized by activity.

- **Lesson Two: Multicellular Specialization Demonstration** *(page 17)*
  Scissors, glue, paper, photocopies of activity

- **Lesson Two: Rock – Paper – Scissors** *(page 18)*
  Small balls of Playdough or plastercine, a piece of paper or pen per student

- **Lesson Three: A Day in the Life of a Uni** *(page 19)*
  Photocopies of worksheet

- **Lesson Four: Cello Jello** *(page 20)*
  Objects to represent organelles, Jello instant powder, bowls

- **Lesson Five: Scrambled Cells** *(page 23)*
  The cell scramble sheet must be photocopied and cut out

- **Lesson Eight: What's Special about Plants?** *(page 26)*
  Photocopies of the organization chart, glued to the back of station cards, and laminated for future use if desired.

- **Lesson Nine: That's Life!** *(page 32)*
  Collect light weight cardboard (the kind found in nylon packages), scissors, markers, string or wool

- **Lesson Ten: Eat, Drink and Be Airy!** *(page 34)*
  Experiment 1 – Paper towels, margarine containers, colored liquid
  Experiment 2 – For each lab group: two healthy plants, masking tape, an eye dropper, plastic wrap, a measuring cup
  Experiment 3 – Each lab group will require plants which are annuals, bienniels and perennials

- **Lesson Eleven: Adept at Adapting** *(page 36)*
  Photocopies of work sheet

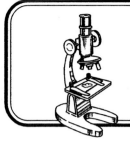

CELLS, TISSUES, ORGANS & SYSTEMS

- **Lesson Thirteen: Experiment – Observing Epithelial Cells** *(page 38)*
  Each lab group will require: a microscope, a slide, a slide cover, blue emthylene, a small tongue depressor or tooth pick, a dropper, and photocopies of the procedure and observation record charts

- **Lesson Fourteen: Experiment – Pass the Salt Please** *(page 40)*
  Each lab group will require: four plants of the same kind, a measuring teaspoon, rock salt, space for plants to remain in favorable light, four old margarine/yogurt containers, a measuring cup, and photocopies of the lab procedures, observation chart and evaluation

- **Lesson Fifteen: A Fair Test?** *(page 43)*
  Photocopies of the handout and work sheet

- **Lesson Sixteen: A Mini-Uni Science Fair** *(page 45)*
  Students will collect their own materials

- **Lesson Seventeen: Neuron Relay** *(page 46)*
  Each group of six to ten students will require paper, pencil and their imagination

- **Lesson Eighteen: Interesting Interdependence** *(page 47)*
  Each partnership will require a source of sugar (candy or pure sugar – not chocolate as it includes a different variable), and a source of caffeine (chocolate or cola), chairs or benches, and access to a stop watch or second hand

- **Lesson Nineteen: Dare to Compare** *(page 48)*
  Photocopies of work sheet

- **Lesson Twenty: Experiment – Let's See How Much 'C'!** *(page 49)*
  Each lab will require one cup of each of the following: orange juice from frozen concentrate, grape juice from concentrate, cranberry juice from concentrate, grapefruit juice from concentrate, fresh orange juice, fresh grape juice, fresh cranberry juice, fresh grapefruit juice. (Note: juices may be substituted as needed.)

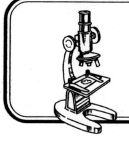

CELLS, TISSUES, ORGANS & SYSTEMS

Bulletin Board Displays

Many of the activities throughout this unit that the students will participate in generate materials suitable for bulletin board display.

If student work is not available, try some of these ideas:

- Turn your bulletin board into a giant plant or animal cell. The bulletin board shape and structure are more conducive to the plant cell.

- Turn your bulletin board into an anatomy lesson on a particular system. Start with the big picture, the plant or animal, and move down through its systems, organs, tissues and cells.

- Use the fact sheet on the history of the cell to create a science in history bulletin board.

History of the Cell
Fact Sheet

In 1665, scientist Robert Hooke called tiny structures seen in cork under a microscope, "cells".

Here are some facts about cells:

- all living things are made of cells, and all life activities of an organism take place in its cells

- an electron microscope can magnify a cell up to 1 000 000 times

- cells come in many shapes and sizes and have many different purposes

- sometimes cells combine together to form a tissue

- tissues group together to form organs

- some things, such as bacteria, have only one cell

- people have trillions of cells

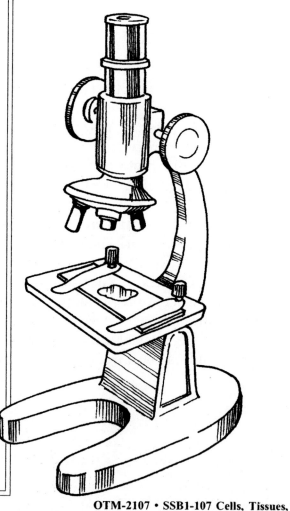

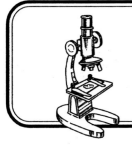

CELLS, TISSUES, ORGANS & SYSTEMS

Evaluation Techniques

The intention of this unit is to be a resource to a homeschool, classroom or rotary science teacher.

Set aside between four and six weeks to complete this unit assuming the students will be working in this subject area at least thirty minutes per day.

Choose ten to fifteen objectives based on your government agency guidelines, board guidelines or school guidelines. Next, choose the combination of activities, seat work selections, and projects which will provide the students with multiple opportunities to meet your selected objectives. Note: If you choose to complete the entire unit, several built-in repeat opportunities for student success have been created.

The activities in this resource may be completed in any order.

The following is a sample evaluation format that you may wish to use:

Quizes	10%
Tests	15%
Lab reports	15%
Work sheets	15%
Projects	15%
Lab work	10%
Presentations	10%
Daily Mark	10%

Using any combination of self, peer and teacher evaluation, the students may be expected to complete a certain number of assignments. (See individual assignments for evaluation samples.)

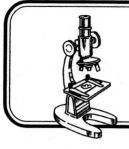

CELLS, TISSUES, ORGANS & SYSTEMS

Lab Rules

1. Work only with the supervision or approval of an adult.

2. Wear safety goggles and some sort of cover (lab coat) for your clothes unless you absolutely know that the substances you are working with will cause no harm.

3. Always assume that what you are working with is dangerous unless you can confirm with an authority otherwise. Therefore it is important to:

    a) Keep substances and organisms away from direct contact with your skin or eyes.

    b) Never eat or taste a substance/organism.

    c) Never inhale deeply around any substance.

4. Make sure you know where safety equipment is in your lab and how to use it in case of an emergency.

5. Ask your supervisor how to dispose of the substances you are working with. Most schools have hazardous waste disposal policies.

6. Wash your hands before and after working in the lab.

7. Maintain an orderly workplace by always returning equipment clean to its appropriate location. An untidy lab may lead to accidents.

8. Report any broken or missing equipment immediately to your supervisor.

CELLS, TISSUES, ORGANS & SYSTEMS

Lesson One: Prokaryotic Cells – Most Unicellular Organisms

Teacher Notes: Prokaryotic cells are simple cells. Their loops of chromosome are not enclosed in a nuclear membrane. Many, but not all, unicellular organisms are prokaryotic but all bacteria are. Some bacteria are necessary for human life while others cause disease. Most bacteria live by absorbing food substances from their surroundings, but some collect energy from sunshine. Bacteria usually reproduce by dividing in two. In the average human body, the number of the body's own cells are outnumbered by bacteria. Most of the bacteria live on the body's surface and are considered to be 'good' bacteria. 'Good' bacteria prevent other bacteria that may be to harmful from establishing themselves.

Vocabulary: Prokaryotic, bacterium/bacteria, amoeba, pseudopod, flagella, protozoans

Hook: Have students brainstorm various modes of locomotion. Next, narrow the application to bacteria and guess which forms of locomotion still apply.

Activity: Students should complete the activity "Locomotion Notion" and take it up. Students should take a brief note based on the information supplied above.

Homework: Students should review the diagrams on the "Locomotion Notion" work sheet and be prepared to complete a quiz based on the labeling of these diagrams. (Note: the label definitions are found in the vocabulary list.)

Suggested Evaluation: Work sheet completed and corrected *(5 marks)*

Quiz on labels *(15 marks)*

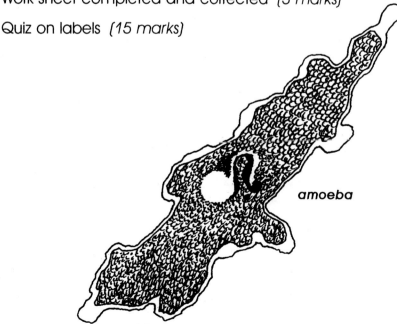

amoeba

Lesson 1

CELLS, TISSUES, ORGANS & SYSTEMS

Locomotion Notion

Name: _____

Single-celled organisms move in different ways:
- flagella
- by spinning
- by flowing or changing shape
- by undulating

Make your best scientific guess as to what form of locomotion each of the following prokaryotic cells uses.

1. Diagram of a Bacterium

Locomotion: ___flagella___

2. Diagram of an Amoeba

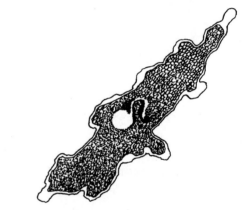

Locomotion: ___by flowing or changing shape___

3. Diagram of a Protozoan

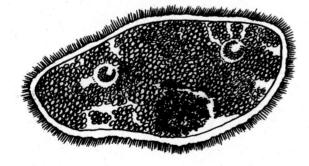

Locomotion: ___by undulating___

4. Diagram of a Ceratium

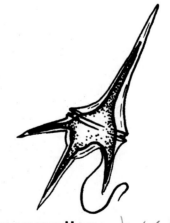

Locomotion: ___by spinning___

Lesson 1

© On The Mark Press • S&S Learning Materials   16   OTM-2107 • SSB1-107 Cells, Tissues, Organs & Systems

 # CELLS, TISSUES, ORGANS & SYSTEMS

Lesson Two: Multicellular Organisms

Teacher Notes: In multicellular organisms, cells are specialized and divide the work, rather than having each cell perform all the same functions. Specialization causes cell differences in structure, according to what is best suited to certain functions. The ability of specialized cells to complete other functions is decreased.

Vocabulary: eukaryotic cells, specialization

Hook: Create a banner with your school name and the word "factory" at the end. Introduce yourself as the plant manager and welcome all of your new employees along. Explain that they are privileged to be part of a group of people all making paper flowers. They each will be responsible for designing and making a 30-cm (12-in) high flower. (These can be used later to decorate your bulletin boards!) Challenge the students to work as quickly as they can. From the moment that you begin, time the process. Periodically tell the students the amount of time that has elapsed so far. Once all of the flowers have been made, announce the total time it took to complete the predetermined number of flowers.

Activities:

1. Specialization Demonstration

Materials: Various colors of paper, scissors and glue

Now, challenge the students to choose the design they like the best. Using this design as a template, divide the members of the class into teams and have each person specialize in a certain part of the flower making process. For example, have one student responsible for making stems, another petals, and yet another leaves. Give the students the same amount of time that it took them in the hook activity. At the end of the allotted time, count the total number of flowers created in the entire class and compare that with the total number of flowers created in the hook activity.

Discussion: Assuming that more flowers were created, discuss the reasons why the second process was more efficient. Relate their answers to the concept of specialization in cells.

Homework: Pose the question, "How does it benefit multicellular organisms to have cell specialization?"

Lesson 2

CELLS, TISSUES, ORGANS & SYSTEMS

2. Rock-Paper-Scissors

Materials: Playdough, a piece of paper or pencil per student

Students will be directed to play Rock-Paper-Scissors. On the count of three, students choose to make either the rock (symbolized by a fist), paper (symbolized by a flat hand, fingers together) or scissors (symbolized by a hand, baby finger to ground with fingers split to form a 'v'). Each time after the decision has been made the students are asked to perform a task. Students may note which tasks their choice of 'hands' are best suited for. Tasks may include: flattening a ball of Playdough, shaking someone's hand, picking up a pencil or piece of paper.

Note: If this hand feature were permanent, it would be a form of specialization or adaptation.

Homework: Brainstorm a list of animals or plants which clearly have a physical specialization for their environment.

Suggested Evaluation: Completion of homework, daily mark for participation in class.

 # CELLS, TISSUES, ORGANS & SYSTEMS

Lesson Three: A Day in the Life of a Uni

Teacher Notes: To focus the students' attention on themselves as a multicellular organism, have them complete the comparison chart between multicellular and unicellular organisms.

Activity: Comparison work sheet below

- -

Cells, Tissues, Organs & Systems   A Day in the Life of a Uni

Name: _____

1. Make a list of all the things you need on a regular basis to survive.

   _____
   _____
   _____
   _____
   _____
   _____

2. Now list the needs of a unicellular organism.

   _____
   _____

3. In what ways are the two similar and in what ways are they different?

   _____
   _____
   _____
   _____
   _____

Lesson 3

CELLS, TISSUES, ORGANS & SYSTEMS

Lesson Four: Cello Jello

Teacher Notes: A multicellular organism holds within its cytoplasm many organelles. These are mini-organs that carry out vital functions for the survival of the cell. Pictures of the finished cello Jello products would make a colorful and informative bulletin board display.

Warning: Be very careful to avoid common allergy-inducing foods with this activity such as nuts, and do survey anyone who may come in contact with the end product for allergies.

Organelles and Other Parts of a Cell

Cytoplasm – a gel-like substance which fills the entire area inside the cell wall or membrane and supports the other organelles

Nucleus – the main organelle; separated by the nuclear membrane and contains DNA (deoxyrobonucleic acid – genetic material)

Cell Membrane – a flexible barrier which surrounds the cytoplasm and organelles, but which may also be permeable to selected substances

Endoplasmic Reticulum – site of protein production; also involved in transport and storage

Mitochondria – responsible for cellular respiration, producing energy to carry out all cell functions

Golgi Apparatus – a collection of sacs that store then release compounds made in the endoplasmic reticulum

Lysosomes – small membranous bags containing digestive enzymes

Ribosomes – particles containing ribonucleic acid (RNA) responsible for making proteins; they are free floating in the cytoplasm but often are found attached to the endoplasmic reticulum

Animal Cell

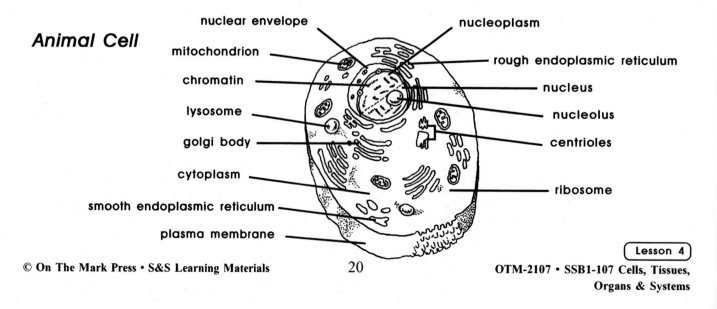

nuclear envelope — nucleoplasm
mitochondrion — rough endoplasmic reticulum
chromatin — nucleus
lysosome — nucleolus
golgi body — centrioles
cytoplasm — ribosome
smooth endoplasmic reticulum
plasma membrane

Lesson 4

CELLS, TISSUES, ORGANS & SYSTEMS

Plant Cell

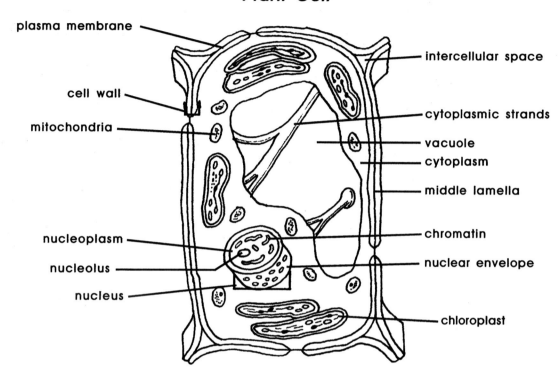

Vocabulary: Cytoplasm, nucleus, cell membrane, endoplasmic reticulum, mitochondria, golgi apparatus, lysosomes, ribosomes

Materials: Students will supply various candy or nonedible objects to represent the organelles of a plant and an animal cell. The teacher will supply, out of the school budget, a package of Jello instant powder for each lab group.

Hook: Explain that you are going to be having a cello Jello contest. Students need to supply the organelles for their animal and plant cells. The teacher will provide the Jello.

Activity: Each lab group will create an animal and a plant cell for either consumption or display. (Be sure to clarify which.)

Homework: Collect all of the organelle supplies needed.

Suggested Evaluation: Students may be evaluated on the basis of their finished product and their contribution to the group. See sample evaluation on page 22.

Lesson 4

CELLS, TISSUES, ORGANS & SYSTEMS

Cello Jello Evaluation Form

Name: _____

Includes Label and Organelle	Out of	Self-Evaluation	Peer Evaluation	Teacher Evaluation	Total	Comment
Cytoplasm	/2					
Nucleus	/2					
Cell Membrane	/2					
Endoplasmic Reticulum	/2					
Mitochondria	/2					
Golgi Apparatus	/2					
Lysosome	/2					
Ribosomes	/2					
Contribution to Group	/9	/25	/25	/25	/25	

 # CELLS, TISSUES, ORGANS & SYSTEMS

Lesson Five: Scrambled Cells

Teacher Notes: Prepare beforehand, or have the students cut out and scramble the contents of the two cell diagrams. Have the students reconstruct both cells and then color and label them. These would make a colorful bulletin board display and they would be an excellent reminder to students about the cell parts.

Vocabulary: Review lessons one to four

_ _

Cells, Tissues, Organs & Systems

Scrambled Cells

Name: _____

Cut out and scramble these two cells. Then, without checking a diagram, unless you have to, try to put them back together again correctly using a blank page as your background.

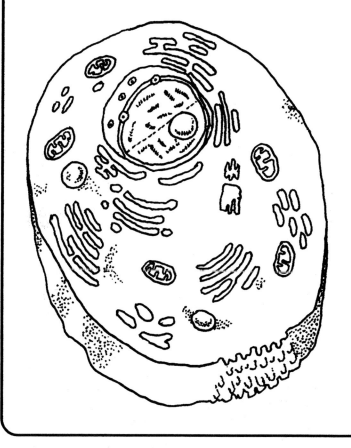

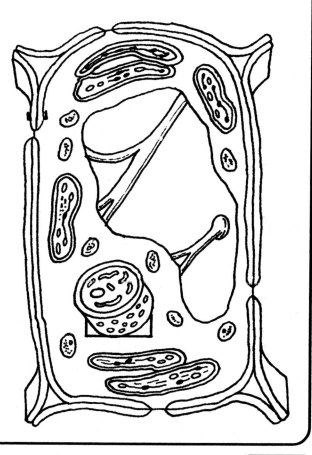

Lesson 5

CELLS, TISSUES, ORGANS & SYSTEMS

Lesson Six: What are Tissues, Organs and Systems?

Teacher Notes: Place the following note on the chalk board, an overhead, or hand out copies of it to students.

Vocabulary: cartilage, connective tissue, epithelial tissue, exocrine, endocrine

What are Tissues, Organs and Systems?

There are four main types of tissues:

1. **Epithelial Tissue** – which covers the body, lines the body cavities and forms glands

2. **Connective Tissue** – which protects and supports the organs and skeletal aspects of the body, binding them together

3. **Muscular Tissue** – which enables the body to move

4. **Nervous Tissue** – which begins, sends and receives nerve impulses to coordinate body activities

Tissues combine together to form organs. For example, the heart is comprised of muscle tissue, which is stimulated by nervous tissue, held in place by connective tissue, and finally internally lined with epithelial tissue. Other organs are similarly constructed (e.g., lungs, liver, brain, kidneys, etc.).

A gland is a particular kind of organ that makes and releases substances into the body. An exocrine gland secretes what it produces (sweat) via a duct. An endocrine gland secretes what it produces (hormones) directly into the bloodstream.

Several organs combine to form a system. For example; the cardiovascular system is comprised of the heart, lungs, and all of the vessels which carry blood. Other systems include the respiratory and digestive systems.

Homework: Have students re-read the note and attempt to learn the spelling of words.

Suggested Evaluation: Daily mark and quiz

Quiz

1. What are the four main types of tissue? *(4 marks for answer + 4 marks for spelling)*
2. Choose one of the tissues and explain where it is found. *(2 marks)*
3. What is a system? *(2 marks - 1 for each component)*
4. Name one kind of gland and define it. *(2 marks for answer + 1 mark for spelling)*

Total   /15   Lesson 6

 # CELLS, TISSUES, ORGANS & SYSTEMS

Lesson Seven: Be Selectively Permeable

Teacher Notes: The exterior wall or plasma membrane of a cell functions as a barrier to some substances and as a gateway to others. Through chemical identification, the cell can change the structure of its membrane (either physically or chemically) to allow passage into the cell. The plasma membrane can be involved in several types of exchanges through its membranes: phagocytosis (the engulfing of food particles), endocytosis (the intake of fluids), or exocytosis (the expulsion of waste products).

Vocabulary: semi-permeable, phagocytosis, engulfing, endocytosis, exocytosis

Activity: Red Rover

To demonstrate this concept to the students, try a game of "Red Rover". Divide the class into two teams. Have the "calling" team (Team A) decide on a shape for their barrier. For example, they may form a traditional link of holding hands. The difference between this and traditional Red Rover is that the line cannot move or obstruct the other team except by the physical shape that they have formed.

The team being "called over" (Team B) decides on a shape for each individual to take on. When Team A calls over a person from Team B, the outcome of whether or not they can move through the line is solely dependent on the compatibility of the shapes that have been chosen. For example, if Team A has formed a traditional link of hands and a member of Team B has decided to crawl when called, the member of Team B would make it through the membrane and therefore not be captured.

Some students may have the tendency to change what they had committed to once they see the membrane. One way to get around this is to have the entire of Team A and B display their postures at the same time. Keep in mind that Team B may choose a locomotor pattern also. For example, if they decide to leap to the line and Team A has somehow linked with their feet, it is possible for the member of Team B to leap over the barrier.

Adapt the game as you like. Good luck and have fun.

Suggested Evaluation: Active participation, daily mark

CELLS, TISSUES, ORGANS & SYSTEMS

Lesson Eight: What's Special about Plants?

Teacher Notes: The following lesson has been designed as a jigsaw activity. It may also be completed as a work station activity or as part of a centers activity. There are five information cards and an information organizer for students to take notes from the cards. The cards may be photocopied, colored and laminated in order to preserve them for future use.

Vocabulary: Ovary, stamen, pistil, carpel, sepel, anther, stigma, style, phloem, xylem, herbacious, epidermis

Hook: Have students consider their own body parts and brainstorm parts which have particular shapes or features for specific functions. (Note: Gage the maturity of your students before attempting this activity.)

Activity: Photocopy, cut out, color and laminate these cards for station use.

Suggested Evaluation: Completion of the Organization Chart *(15 marks)*

Roots

Description:

Roots anchor plants to the ground, absorb water and absorb minerals. Roots generally grow down or in the same direction as gravity. Roots are generally covered in tiny hairs which serve to increase the surface area through which water and nutrients may be absorbed.

Internally, roots have two main features, xylem and phloem.

Specialized Function:

Some roots act as fuel storage such as beets and carrots.

Some roots help to stabilize the stem of the plant such as with *Epphytes* (a tropical tree).

CELLS, TISSUES, ORGANS & SYSTEMS

Stems

Description:

Stems usually grow upward against gravity. They have nodes along their surface to which leaves are attached in a regular pattern.

Stems are quite variable in their appearance. Structurally, they have three tissue systems. In woody plants there is xylem and phloem in the stem whereas in waxy or soft plants there is parenchyma tissue and phloem.

Specialized Function:

Modifications of the plant include thorns, climbing stems, photosynthetic properties in the absence of leaves, creepers, underground food storage (tulips).

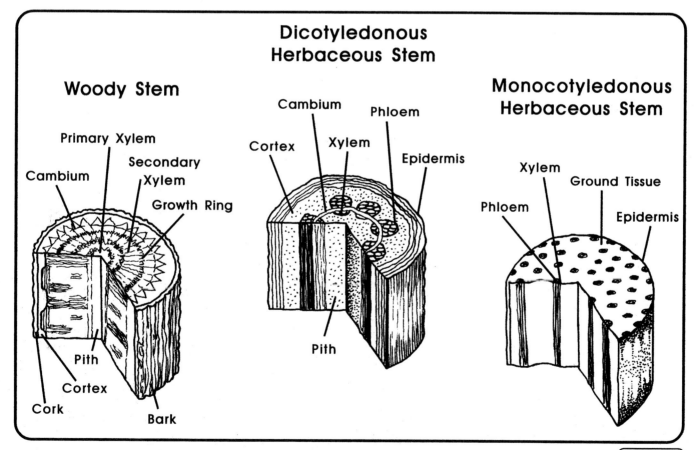

Dicotyledonous Herbaceous Stem

Woody Stem

Monocotyledonous Herbaceous Stem

Woody Stem labels: Primary Xylem, Secondary Xylem, Growth Ring, Cambium, Pith, Cortex, Cork, Bark

Dicotyledonous Herbaceous Stem labels: Cambium, Phloem, Cortex, Xylem, Epidermis, Pith

Monocotyledonous Herbaceous Stem labels: Xylem, Ground Tissue, Phloem, Epidermis

Leaves

Description:

Photosynthesis is the primary function of leaves for most plants. Leaves are usually made up of parenchyma tissue. This tissue consists of loosely spaced cells to aid in the exchange of carbon dioxide and oxygen. The leaf has a vascular system which moves water and food products to other parts of the plant.

The part of the leaf which connects it to the stem is called the petiole.

Specialized Function:

Some leaves help protect plants from predators through their spiny protrusions. Some plants have leaves which trap and digest insects. Other leaves attract insects to pollinate through their bright colors.

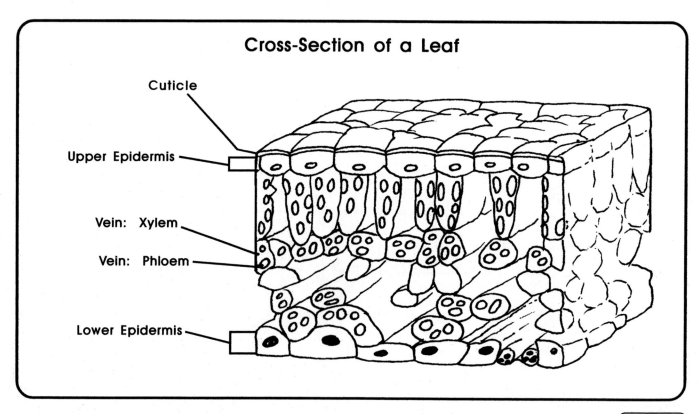

Cross-Section of a Leaf

Cuticle

Upper Epidermis

Vein: Xylem

Vein: Phloem

Lower Epidermis

Lesson 8

Flowers

Description:

Flowers are essentially leaves which are modified to serve the special function of reproduction.

Specialized Function:

Every flower is the end of a stem-like structure. The flower itself is several layers deep. The outermost layer is called the calyx, and it is a couple of greeny petals which protect the flower bud before it opens. Next from the outside in, is the corolla. This is the colorful portion we see. It consists of petals and is nectar producing. The next layer in consists of stamens that produce the pollen necessary for reproduction. The innermost portion is the pistil. Pistils are made of carpels and these in turn contain at least one ovary. Each ovary has ovules (immature seeds) attached.

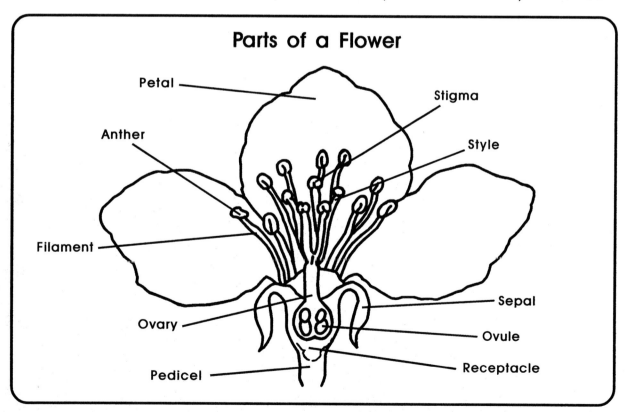

Parts of a Flower

Lesson 8

Fruits

Description:

Fruit is essentially the mature ovary of a flowering plant.

Usually, fruit is produced after the plant's ovules have been fertilized. However, today we cultivate many fruits such as seedless citrus fruits, bananas, and cucumbers without fertilization.

Specialized Function:

The major function of fruit in plants is to protect the maturing seeds. However in some plants the fruit also serves as a means of distributing seeds.

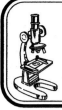 

CELLS, TISSUES, ORGANS & SYSTEMS

What's Special about Plants?

Organization Chart

Name: _____

Plant Part	Description	Function	Diagram
Roots			
Stems			
Leaves			
Flowers			
Fruits			

Lesson 8

 # CELLS, TISSUES, ORGANS & SYSTEMS

Lesson Nine: That's Life!

Teacher Notes: Cells in humans reproduce themselves in two different ways.

a) **Meiosis** – the division of reproductive cells to produce sperm and ovum; begins with one primary cell and creates four cells with half the original number of chromosomes.

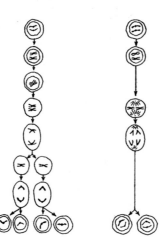

b) **Mitosis** – the division of all other cells; it begins with one primary cell and results in two identical cells.

Vocabulary: mitosis, meiosis, zygote, spermatozoa, oocytes, ovum

Materials: colored paper, scissors, glue

Hook: Pyramid Building. With cards, blocks, people. When you're done, label as follows.

—   (primary spermatocyte)

— —   (secondary spermatocytes)

— — — —   (spermatids)

— — — — — — — —   (spermatozoa)

Activity: Make cut-out discs of different colors and create labeled models for meiosis and mitosis in your notebooks.

Homework: Review the diagram so that students are able to distinguish mitosis from meiosis and describe the purpose of each.

Suggested Evaluation: Quiz *(6 marks)*

CELLS, TISSUES, ORGANS & SYSTEMS

That's Life! Evaluation

Name: _____

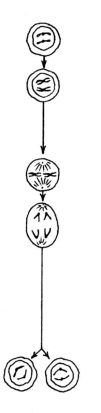
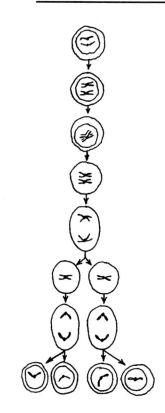

1. This is a diagram of _____
   (1 mark)

2. This is a diagram of _____
   (1 mark)

3. What is the purpose of mitosis? *(2 marks)*

_____

_____

_____

4. What is the purpose of meiosis? *(2 marks)*

_____

_____

_____

CELLS, TISSUES, ORGANS & SYSTEMS

Lesson Ten: Eat, Drink and Be Airy!

Teacher Notes: Divide the class into three groups and have each one work on a different lab. When the labs are complete, have each group present their lab, including the results, to the other two groups. This can be done as a whole class or in groups of three. The three labs demonstrate the concepts of how a plant's structure permits the movement of food, water and gases. The students may require some assistance extrapolating the results to plant function in general.

Vocabulary: osmosis, diffusion, capillary action

Hook: Discuss the concepts of osmosis and diffusion. Have students look up the terms on their vocabulary lists and attempt to hypothesize how this relates to real plant life.

Activities:

Experiment One: Plants move water and food through tubes in the middle of the stem. Food, water and gases must be brought into the cell and removed from the cell. These substances are moved through plants by what is called capillary action.

Materials: Margarine container or cup, food coloring, sugar, salt, napkin or paper towel

Procedure:

1. Fill a cup half full with water and add a drop of food coloring.
2. Place a paper towel hanging half into the water and half over the edge of the cup.
3. Create a chart and record your observations.
4. Repeat the experiment with a sugar and water mixture.
5. Repeat the experiment with a salt and water mixture.
6. Does the temperature of the solution make any difference?
7. Is there a limit to how high the water will climb? Try a higher container.
8. Use materials other than paper towel to determine if one is faster or more effective than another.

Question: How does the action of the water and the paper towel relate to the movement of food, water and gases in a tree?

Experiment Two: If plants transpire (breathing for plants) at night, what happens to the moisture which is expelled as a by-product of their transpiration? Compare the moisture use of two plants.

Materials: Two plants of the same kind and size, masking tape, eye dropper, plastic wrap, measuring cup

Procedure:
1. Control (make sure it is exactly the same) the light, temperature and potting conditions.
2. Each night, cover one of the plants with plastic wrap.
3. Each day, uncover the plant and record the general health of the plant (e.g., wilting, growth, color)
4. Construct a log to record your observations over the time period of one week.
5. Repeat the experiment in cold and hot conditions.
6. Repeat the experiment while maintaining a light source on both plants twenty-four hours a day.

Questions: What factors affect transpiration in plants?
Do plants collect their own wet by-product for use?

Experiment Three: Different plants have different sizes of vascular tubes. Plants of different ages have tubes of different ages. Will older plants have larger, smaller, greater or lesser vascular tubes than younger ones?

Materials: Each lab group will need annuals (plants with a one-year life span), biennials (plants with a two-year life span), and perennials (plants which grow every year without intervention), water, food coloring and three glasses

Procedures:
1. Place each plant in turn in a glass labeled and filled with colored water.
2. Determine the age of the plants by the number of vascular tubes the colored water exposes.

Questions: How can one determine the age of a perennial?
Do plants grow from the inside out or the outside in?

 # CELLS, TISSUES, ORGANS & SYSTEMS

Lesson Eleven: Adept at Adapting

Teacher Notes: All organisms are structurally adapted to the needs of their environment. This includes the need to obtain energy and water and to fight off or discourage predators. For example, the giraffe has a long neck to reach the scarce foliage on the top of trees in grass scrubland.

Vocabulary: Review other vocabulary.

Hook: Have students discuss various adaptations with which they are familiar.

Activity: Have students complete the chart on plant adaptations.

Suggested Evaluation: Completion of Adept at Adapting *(16 marks)*

- -

Cells, Tissues, Organs & Systems   Adept at Adapting

Name: _____

Complete the following chart.

Plant	Feature One and Reason for It	Feature Two and Reason for It
Cactus		
Palm Tree		
Grass		
Your choice:		

 # CELLS, TISSUES, ORGANS & SYSTEMS

Lesson Twelve: Osmosis and Diffusion

Teacher Notes: Osmosis is the movement of water molecules from an area of higher concentration to an area of lower concentration through a semi-permeable membrane. Diffusion is the passive movement of a substance from a region of higher concentration to an area of lower concentration until an equilibrium develops.

Vocabulary: osmosis, diffusion, equilibrium

Activity: Have students develop an activity in lab groups to demonstrate one of the concepts of osmosis or diffusion.

Suggested Evaluation: Demonstrates concept clearly *(3 marks)*

Write up for demonstration including the objective, materials, procedure, conclusions, and marks for spelling and grammar *(10 marks)*

Presentation – speak clearly, explain clearly, use of objects to help explain *(3 marks)*

Lesson 12

CELLS, TISSUES, ORGANS & SYSTEMS

Lesson Thirteen: The Microscope

Teacher Notes: The microscope requires special care and instructions for use. Be sure to cover the microscope rules with the students prior to their using the equipment. The following activity will introduce the students to the microscope as part of a lab.
Note: Blue methylene can be purchased through any science supplier.

Vocabulary: Epithelial cells, buccal

Hook: Answer the question, "What do you think the mucous on the inside of your mouth is made of?"

Activity:

Experiment: Observing epithelial cells lining the buccal cavity

The following microscope rules must be followed at all times in the lab.

1. Always carry a microscope with two hands. Put one under the stage and with the other, grasp the arm.
2. Always return the lens to the lowest power (the smallest one).
3. Always return the microscope to its proper storage place after use.
4. Start from the smallest power. Then slowly and carefully work your way up until you have your object in focus.

Materials: A slide, a slide cover, blue methylene, a dropper and a small tongue depressor or toothpick

Procedure:
1. Using a small clean scraper, take a swab of the lining of the inside of your cheek.
2. Spread the whitish mucous thinly on the slide.
3. Wait approximately three to five minutes for it to dry out, then put one drop of blue methylene on the slide.
4. Wait another three to five minutes before rinsing the slide gently under a trickle of water to remove excess blue methylene.
5. Place a slide cover over your sample.
6. Place the slide on the microscope platform with the lens on the smallest setting.
7. Adjust the focus knob until you are able to observe the blue cells.

Name: _____

Experiment - Epithelial Cells

Observations:

1. Draw a picture here of everything you can see in the microscope lens.

2. Now describe in words what you see.

_____

_____

3. Now look at this diagram of a typical animal cell. Use the space provided to compare what you see in the microscope to this diagram.

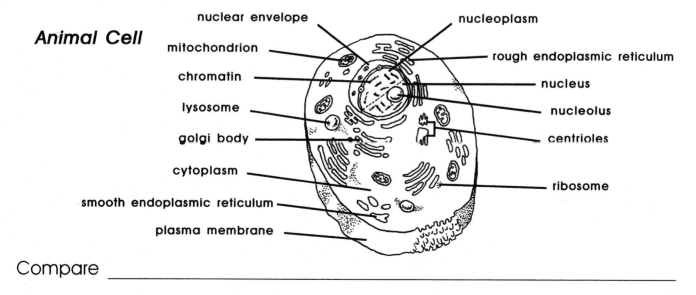

Animal Cell

nuclear envelope

nucleoplasm

mitochondrion

rough endoplasmic reticulum

chromatin

nucleus

lysosome

nucleolus

golgi body

centrioles

cytoplasm

ribosome

smooth endoplasmic reticulum

plasma membrane

Compare _____

_____

CELLS, TISSUES, ORGANS & SYSTEMS

Lesson Fourteen: Pass the Salt Please

Teacher Notes: This lesson focuses on the students' ability to form a hypothesis, and design and conduct an experiment. A tropism is a response a plant has to a stimulus. There are many types of tropisms:

Chemotropism	– a response to chemicals
Thigmotropism	– a response to touch
Thermotropism	– a response to heat
Phototropism	– a response to light
Hydrotopism	– a response to water
Geotropism	– a response to gravity

Vocabulary: tropism, qualitative, quantitative, hypothesis

Expectations: Students will follow procedures as outlined in the lab.
Students will collect qualitative and quantitative data.
Students will know the difference between qualitative and quantitative data.
Students will complete a partial write up of a formal lab.

Suggested Lab Report Evaluation:

Evidence of procedures being followed
(four plants and four watering preparations)   *(8 marks)*

Completion of observation chart (a quarter-mark each)   *(20 marks)*

Completion of accurate description in sentence   *(3 marks)*
form and good copy

Conclusion in sentence form   *(2 Marks)*

Question answered in sentence form   *(2 Marks)*

Total *(35 marks)*

Extension Activity:

Students may create their own experiment based on one of the tropisms.
Design and complete a formal write up on the experiment.

CELLS, TISSUES, ORGANS & SYSTEMS

Activity:

Experiment: What Is the Effect of Salt on Plant Growth?

Hypothesis: Salt will adversely affect plant growth.

Equipment:
- four plants of the same kind
- rock salt (used on ice and snow)
- four old margarine/yogurt containers
- a measuring cup
- a measuring teaspoon
- space for plants to be stored in favorable light

Procedure:

1. Place four similar houseplants in a spot which is conducive to growth (ample light and moderate temperature).

2. Label each of the margarine containers from one to four.

3. In three of the four margarine containers, create different strength solutions of salt and water.

4. In container one, place three teaspoons of rock salt in three cups of water. In container two, mix two teaspoons of rock salt in three cups of water. In container three, mix one teaspoon of rock salt in three cups of water. In container four, place three cups of water. (Container four is what is called the control situation as the plant receives what is considered normal conditions.)

5. Label each plant with the number 1,2,3, or 4.

6. Water the plants once per day using the corresponding solution number for each plant. Stir the solutions before you water with them, ten times each.

7. Water each plant a set amount every time (for example, half a cup).

8. Continue this protocol for two weeks, recording daily the measurement and appearance of each plant on the chart provided.

 # CELLS, TISSUES, ORGANS & SYSTEMS

Name: _____

Experiment - What Is the Effect of Salt on Plant Growth?

	Plant One		Plant Two		Plant Three		Plant Four	
	Measurement Height/Width	Observation	Measurement Height/Width	Observation	Measurement Height/Width	Observation	Measurement Height/Width	Observation
Day 1								
Day 2								
Day 3								
Day 4								
Day 5								
Day 6								
Day 7								
Day 8								
Day 9								
Day 10								
Total								
Day 10-1								
Subtract								

Description of results: _____

_____

_____

Conclusion: _____

_____

_____

Question: What kind of tropism does this experiment represent? _____

_____

_____

Lesson 14

 # CELLS, TISSUES, ORGANS & SYSTEMS

Lesson Fifteen: A Fair Test?

Teacher Notes: Students can receive this information in the form of a board note, overhead or photocopied hand out. Then they will put this information to use to design a fair test of their own.

Vocabulary: variable, valid, fair test, bias

A Fair Test?

In order to design a fair test there are several basic considerations.

Firstly, the variables in the experiment must be limited. For example, if you want to look at the effects of temperature on mold growth in bread, then you must make sure that all objects in your sample are subjected to the same moisture levels and light levels. In addition, you must ensure that the bread is initially of the same age.

Secondly, you must remove any bias or preconceived perceptions about how your investigation will turn out. One way of removing such bias is to design your experiment in a manner that will yield quantitative (numerical data) results. Another method of removing bias when dealing with subjects (specimens or humans) is to take a random sampling. For example, if all of the participants are somehow labeled and each label is placed on a card, you could shuffle the deck and draw any number of cards for a random sample. When a random sampling has not been used, sometimes the investigator's preferences for some characteristic will become evident in their selection of experimental subjects.

Finally, the validity of your test must be optimized. In order to do this the likelihood of your results occurring by chance must be diminished. By including in your investigation as many tests or trials as is possible given time, money and space limitations, you will have done all you can to design a fair test.

 # CELLS, TISSUES, ORGANS & SYSTEMS

Name: _____

A Fair Test?

Activity: Choose one of the questions below and create a fair test.

- Are facts that are learned just before sleep remembered better than those learned at other times of the day?
- Does background noise affect memory?
- Do odors affect memorization?
- Does music affect task performance?
- Do teacher expectations of success or failure affect student results?
- Is one eye of greater importance then the either eye when presented with a visual memory exercise?
- Do females achieve strength or muscle girth increase similar to males by following the same training regiments?

1. What variables need to be controlled?
   _____

2. How will you control the variables?
   _____

3. How will you ensure there is no experimenter bias?
   _____

4. How will you ensure the test is valid (the test is testing what you wanted and can be repeated)?
   _____

5. What is your hypothesis?
   _____

6. What are the materials needed?
   _____

7. What are your experimental procedures?
   _____

 # CELLS, TISSUES, ORGANS & SYSTEMS

Lesson Sixteen: A Mini-Uni Fair

Teacher Notes: This lesson is an opportunity for your students to creatively express what they have learned. Provide a variety of materials such as pipe cleaners, string, construction paper, cardboard, coat hangers, etc. and let them create!

Vocabulary: Review of previous vocabulary

Activity: Design and create a model of a unicellular organism. The model must be three-dimensional and accurate. The organism must also have a cue card type placard attached to it on which the name and a description of the uni is found.

Homework: Research the uni to be created.

Suggested Evaluation: Have students generate criteria for the evaluation of this project with teacher approval.

CELLS, TISSUES, ORGANS & SYSTEMS

Lesson Seventeen: Neuron Relay

Teacher Notes: This relay game is a demonstration of the nervous system at work.

The nervous system receives and interprets stimuli, and relays messages to organs to have a specific responsive outcome. There are two components of the nervous system

a) Neurons – highly specialized cells that conduct nerve impulses over distances (long and skinny cells)

b) Neuroglia – provide protection and nutrition for the nerve cell, and help transmit signals

Vocabulary: neurons, neuroglia

Physical Education
Activity: Neuron Relay

Materials: small piece of paper at the head of each neuron (relay team)

How to Play: Divide the class into relay teams of about ten people each. Divide each team in half and have them line up one behind the other with the head of each line facing the other line. Each line represents a neuron. Place a small piece of paper at the head of each neuron. Pass the paper hand to hand until each reaches the end of the neuron. The person at the end of the neuron must bridge the gap between their line and their team's second line by acting out (charade) the word written on the piece of paper. The receiver cannot talk, but must guess by writing down the charade answer on his or her piece of paper. If the answer is correct, the message continues to be passed down the line to the end of the second team.

Here a new message is created. The two players in the middle go to the end of the opposite lines while the new message races towards the synapse.

The winning team completes the relay back to their starting position.

Discussion: Compare the passing of messages across the synapses of neurons to the passing of messages across the gap in the relay team. How are the two similar?

CELLS, TISSUES, ORGANS & SYSTEMS

Lesson Eighteen: Interesting Interdependence

Teacher Notes: Like a finely tuned machine, all of the systems in the human body are intricately interdependent. Screen your students before participating in this activity for any medical conditions which may make participation difficult.

The resting heart rate is best taken upon awakening in the morning, but for lab purposes have students lie down comfortably at rest for ten minutes prior to recording their heart rates. (Note: Do not take a pulse check using your thumb as it has a pulse of its own.)

Vocabulary: interdependence

Activity: What is the effect of exercise on:
- the respiratory system?
- the digestive system?
- the cardiovascular system?

No eating within a half hour prior to this experiment. Use a fair sample of class as subjects.

Student's Name	Resting Heart Rate	Step Up for One Minute	Heart Rate	Post-Exercise Heart Rate (One minute later)

Copy the chart above and repeat the experiment after each subject has rested at least 24 hours. Use the first data collected as a base line and repeat the experiment after each subject has ingested some pure sugar. Wait another 24 hours and have each subject first ingest some caffeine (a cola, or some chocolate) before repeating the test.

Compare your results on all three charts.

Make a statement about the relationship between each of these three systems.

Lesson 18

 # CELLS, TISSUES, ORGANS & SYSTEMS

Lesson Nineteen: Dare to Compare

Teacher Notes: While plants transpire, taking in carbon dioxide and expiring oxygen, animals respire, breathing in oxygen and expiring carbon dioxide.

Vocabulary: transpiration, respiration

Activity: How do the respiratory systems of plants and animals compare?

- -

Cells, Tissues, Organs & Systems   Dare to Compare

Name: _____

	Plant Gases Exchange System	Animal Gases Exchange System
Organs/Organelles Involved		
Gases Involved		
Inspired		
Expired		
Other		

Lesson 19

 # CELLS, TISSUES, ORGANS & SYSTEMS

Lesson Twenty: Let's See How Much 'C'!

Teacher Notes: Researchers are able to do various tests to determine the nutritional content of various foods. Based on this research, food labels, recommended daily consumption levels and disease prevention work is studied. Indophenol can be purchased from any science supply store.

Activity: Experiment - Let's See How Much 'C'!

- -

Cells, Tissues, Organs & Systems   Let's See How Much 'C'!

Name: _____

Question: What kind of fruit juice is the best source of vitamin C?

Hypothesis: _____

_____

Materials:
- Frozen grape, orange and grapefruit juices. Fresh grape, orange and grapefruit juices
- Indophenol (a blue dye sensitive to vitamin C)
- Eye dropper
- Microscope or magnifying glass
- Eight slides
- Slide cover

Procedure:
1. Select a comparable sample of juices controlling for all but one variable.
2. Place one drop on a slide, cover with a slide slip and view under a microscope.
3. Place one drop of indophenol in a teaspoon of juice and stir. Then smear this mixture on a slide.
4. Using a microscope, record your observations by drawing a diagram for each slide and completing the chart on the following page.

Percent of slide stained:

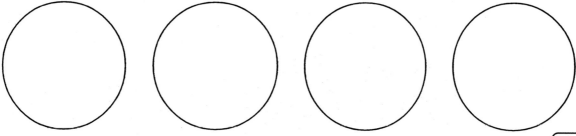

Lesson 20

 # CELLS, TISSUES, ORGANS & SYSTEMS

Name: _____

Let's See How Much 'C'!

Orange Juice from Frozen	Observations	Fresh Orange Juice	Observations
Grape Juice from Frozen	Observations	Fresh Grape Juice	Observations
Cranberry Juice from Frozen	Observations	Fresh Cranberry Juice	Observations
Grapefruit Juice from Frozen	Observations	Fresh Grapefruit Juice	Observations

CELLS, TISSUES, ORGANS & SYSTEMS

Lesson Twenty-One: An Altered State of Cell

Teacher Notes: Insulin decreases blood sugar levels by stimulating transportation of glucose into the liver for storage as glycogen and stimulating glucose uptake by body cells. A lack of insulin results in a number of clinical symptoms referred to as diabetes mellitus.

Vocabulary: Review of previous vocabulary

Activity: Have a special guest speaker come in from your local diabetes foundation to talk to the students about the disease, its causes and treatments, and how they can raise funds to help support research for a cure.

Alternatively, have the students survey the incidence of diabetes in their family or another group of people.

Lesson Twenty-Two: Blood Pressure

Teacher Notes: Blood pressure is a measure of the pressure of circulating blood against the walls of the arteries. Blood pressure is measured at two points: the point at which the heart contracts to empty its blood into the circulation, called systole, and the low point at which the heart relaxes to fill with blood returned by the circulation, called diastole. Pressure is measured in millimeters of mercury by an instrument called a sphygmomanometer. This instrument is made of a cuff that wraps around the upper arm and which is inflated by squeezing a rubber bulb connected to it by a tube. The arm is monitored by a stethoscope applied to an artery in the lower arm. As the cuff expands, it gradually compresses the artery. When the cuff stops the circulation, no pulsations can be heard by the stethoscope. This point is read as the systolic pressure. After, the cuff is gradually deflated until the blood is flowing smoothly again and no further spurting sound is heard. Another reading is taken at this point and is called the diastolic pressure.

In healthy persons, blood pressure increases from about 80/45 in infants, to about 120/80 at age 30, to about 140/85 at age 40 and over. This increase occurs because the arteries lose their elasticity.

Vocabulary: Systole, diastolic, sphygmomanometer

Activity: Invite a public health nurse in to help the students assess their blood pressure. Have students perform various tasks, such as running on the spot, or checking immediately after eating lunch to note the variables that effect blood pressure.

CELLS, TISSUES, ORGANS & SYSTEMS

Bacterium

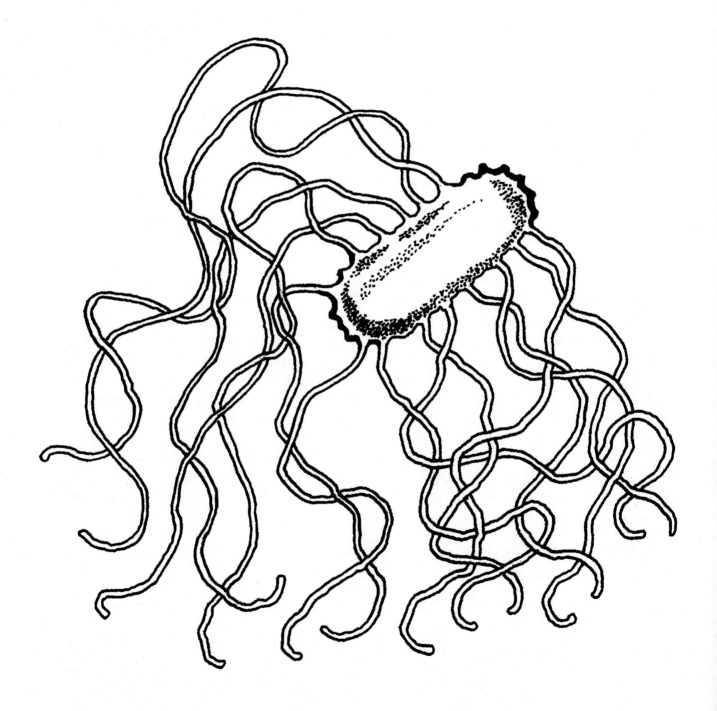

© On The Mark Press • S&S Learning Materials

OTM-2107 • SSB1-107 Cells, Tissues, Organs & Systems

CELLS, TISSUES, ORGANS & SYSTEMS

Amoeba

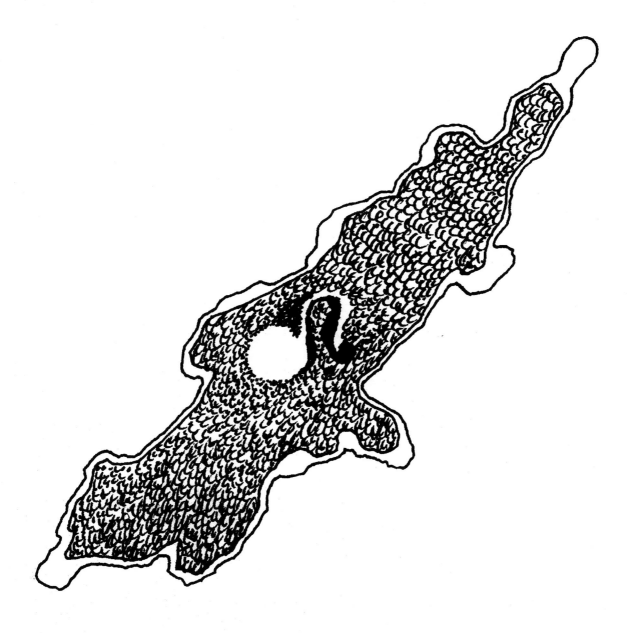

OTM-2107 • SSB1-107 Cells, Tissues, Organs & Systems

CELLS, TISSUES, ORGANS & SYSTEMS

Protozoan

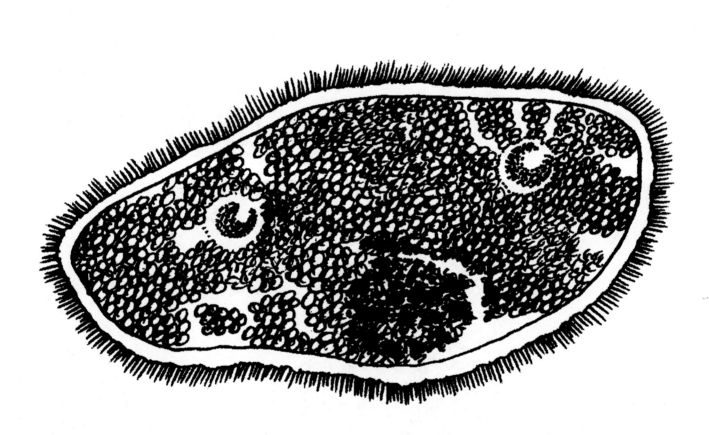

© On The Mark Press • S&S Learning Materials

OTM-2107 • SSB1-107 Cells, Tissues,
Organs & Systems

Cells, Tissues, Organs & Systems

Ceratium

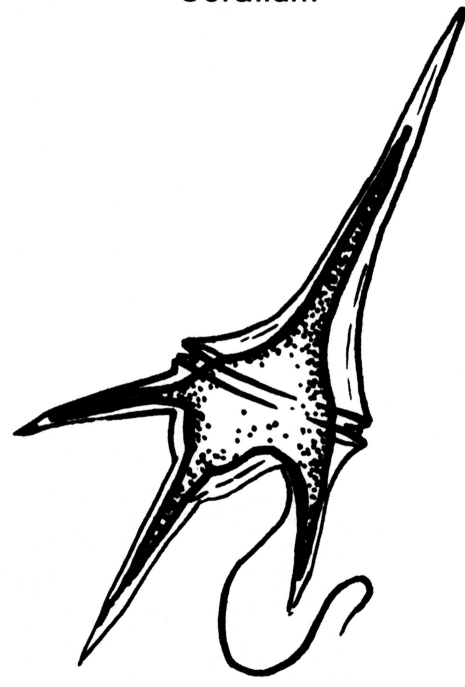

Overhead #4

OTM-2107 • SSB1-107 Cells, Tissues, Organs & Systems

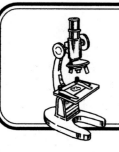

Animal Cell

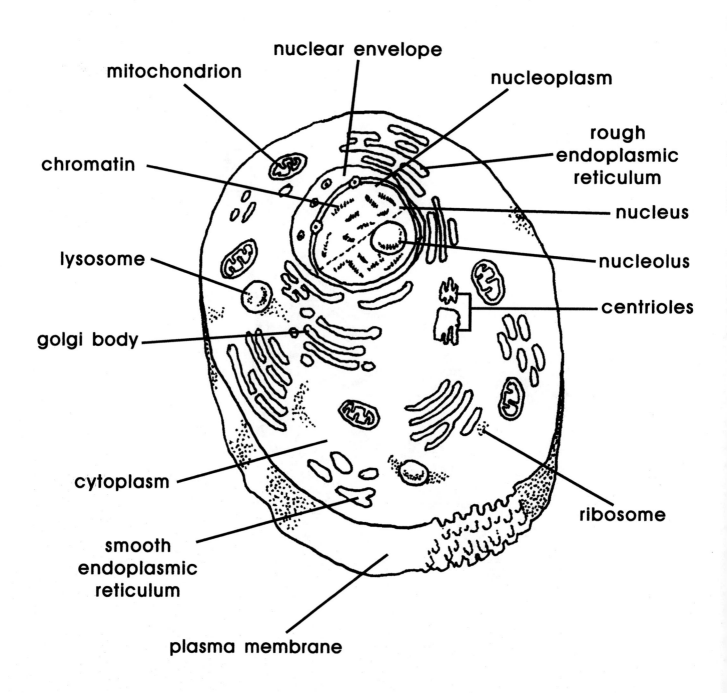

© On The Mark Press • S&S Learning Materials

OTM-2107 • SSB1-107 Cells, Tissues, Organs & Systems

Plant Cell

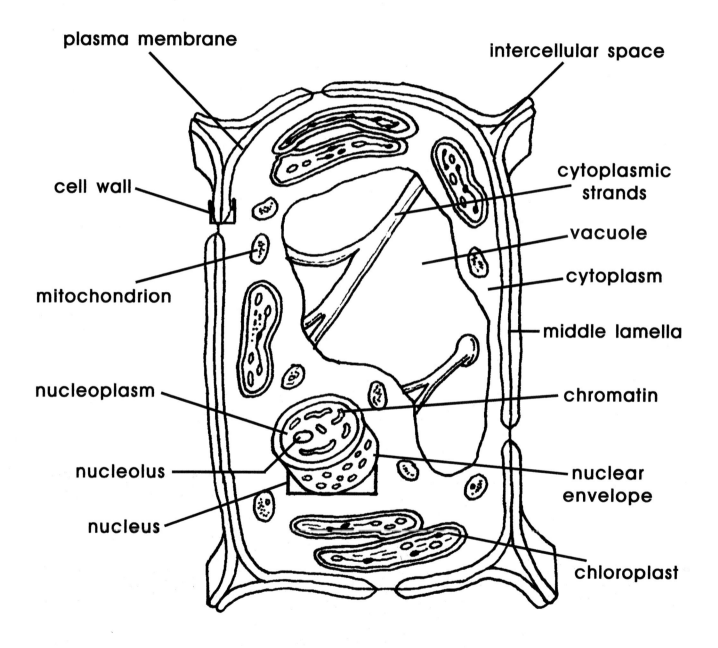

plasma membrane

intercellular space

cell wall

cytoplasmic strands

vacuole

cytoplasm

mitochondrion

middle lamella

nucleoplasm

chromatin

nucleolus

nuclear envelope

nucleus

chloroplast

OTM-2107 • SSB1-107 Cells, Tissues, Organs & Systems

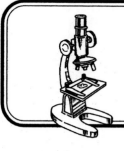

Stems

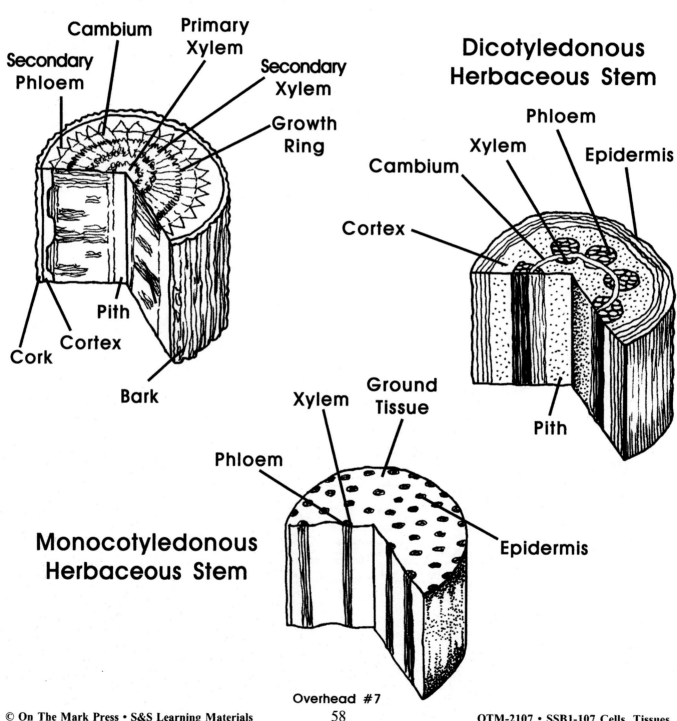

Woody Stem

Secondary Phloem
Cambium
Primary Xylem
Secondary Xylem
Growth Ring
Pith
Cortex
Cork
Bark

Dicotyledonous Herbaceous Stem

Phloem
Xylem
Epidermis
Cambium
Cortex
Pith

Monocotyledonous Herbaceous Stem

Phloem
Xylem
Ground Tissue
Epidermis

Overhead #7

CELLS, TISSUES, ORGANS & SYSTEMS

Cross-Section of a Leaf

Cuticle

Upper Epidermis

Vein: Xylem

Vein: Phloem

Lower Epidermis

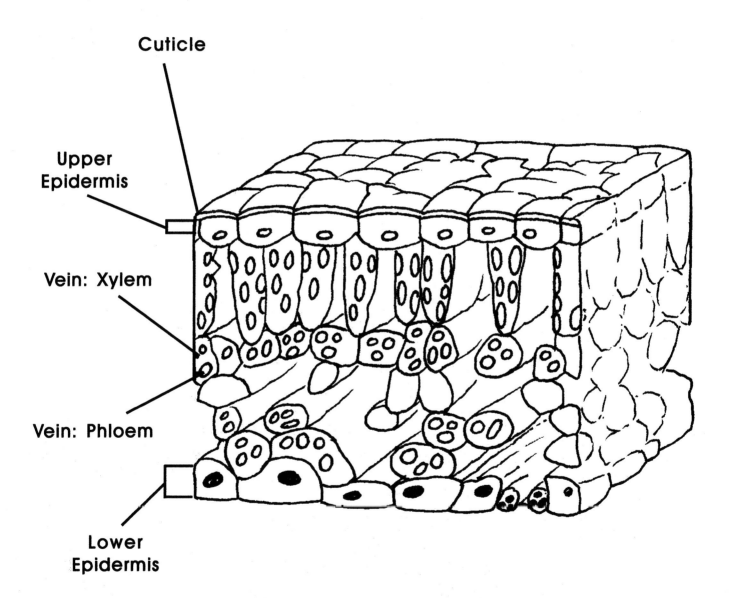

Overhead #8

OTM-2107 • SSB1-107 Cells, Tissues, Organs & Systems

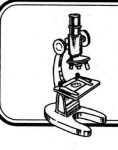

Parts of a Flower

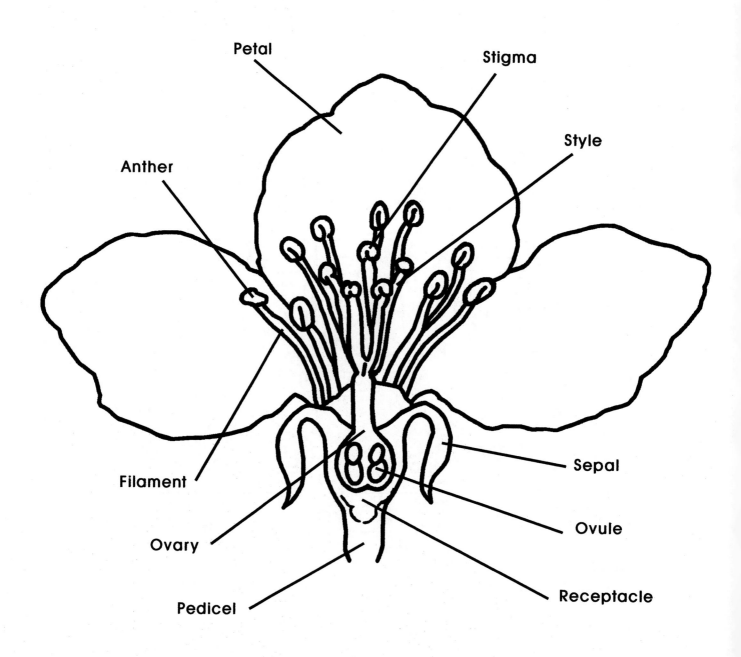

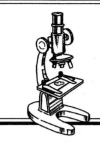

Meiosis

Mitosis

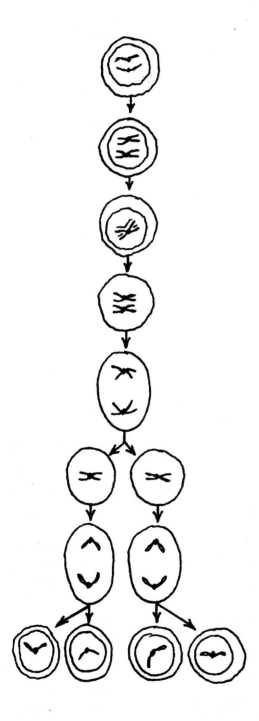

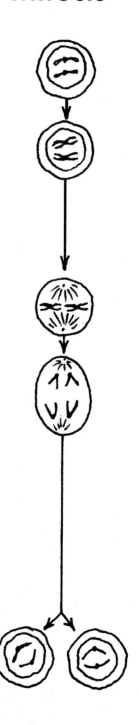

Overhead #10

_____

_____

_____

_____

_____

_____

_____

_____

_____

_____

_____

_____

_____

_____

_____

_____

_____

_____

_____

_____

_____

_____

_____

_____

_____

_____

_____

_____

Answer Key

Lesson One: Locomotion, Notion *(page 16)*
1. *Bacterium:* flagella propel it along
2. *Amoeba:* flows and changes shape
3. *Protozoan:* undulates
4. *Ceratium:* spins

Lesson Three: A Day in the Life of a Uni *(page 19)*
1. Things we need include: water, a source of energy, warmth, oxygen, a sense of hope.
2. A unicellular organism requires water, nutrients, oxygen or some other source of energy.
3. It is our capacity to think which makes the need for hope a factor in our survival. This has been demonstrated through various stories of survival and loss in the World Wars' Prisoner of War Camps and in emergency survival situations.

Lesson Five: Scrambled Cells *(page 23)*

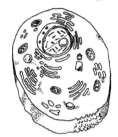 

Lesson Six: Quiz *(page 24)*
1. epithelial tissue, connective tissue, muscular tissue, nervous tissue
2. *One of the following is required:*
   - Muscular tissue - found around skeleton and in some organs
   - Nervous tissue - brain, spinal column, and nerves (spread throughout the body)
   - Connective tissue - found around organs and the skeleton
   - Epithelial tissue - covers the body, lines body cavities and forms glands
3. A system is a collection of organs and tissues that work together.
4. *One of the following is required:*
   - Endocrine gland - secretes directly into blood stream
   - Exocrine gland - secretes via a duct

Lesson Eight: What's Special About Plants? *(page 31)*
Students copy information from the center cards - roots, stems, leaves, flowers, fruits
(see pages 26 to 30)

Lesson Nine: That's Life! Evaluation *(page 33)*
1. mitosis
2. meiosis
3. The purpose of mitosis is cell division that begins with one primary cell and results in two identical cells.
4. The purpose of meiosis is the division of reproductive cells to produce sperm and ovum. It begins with one primary cell and creates four cells with half the original number of chromosomes.

Lesson Ten: Eat, Drink and Be Airy:

Experiment One: *(page 34)*
The paper towel demonstrates the capillary action that enables fluid and nourishment to move against gravity in a tree.

Experiment Two: *(page 35)*
Temperature and humidity affect transpiration. Yes, plants collect their own water.

Experiment Three: *(page 35)*
The age of a perennial can be determined by the number of vascular bundles or rings.   Plants grow from the inside out.

Lesson Eleven: Adept at Adapting *(page 36)*
Cactus – spikes ward off predators; spikes maximize surface area to collect moisture
Palm Tree – tall to minimize ground predation of fruit; wide, flat leaves maximize surface area for transpiration
Grass – individual root system maximizes stability of plant, single blade increases efficiency of capillary action

Lesson Twelve: Osmosis and Diffusion *(page 37)*
Answers may vary.

Lesson Fourteen: What Is the Effect of Salt on Plant Growth? *(page 42)*
This experiment represents a chemotropism.

Lesson Fifteen: A Fair Test? *(page 44)*
Answers may vary.

Lesson Nineteen: Dare to Compare *(page 48)*

Organs/ Organelles	leaves, stem, sylem, phloem	lungs, skin, gills nose, mouth
Gases Involved	oxygen, carbon dioxide	oxygen, carbon dioxide
Inspired	carbon dioxide	oxygen
Expired	oxygen	carbon dioxide